'WE ALL WANT TO SETTLE'

But on whose terms?

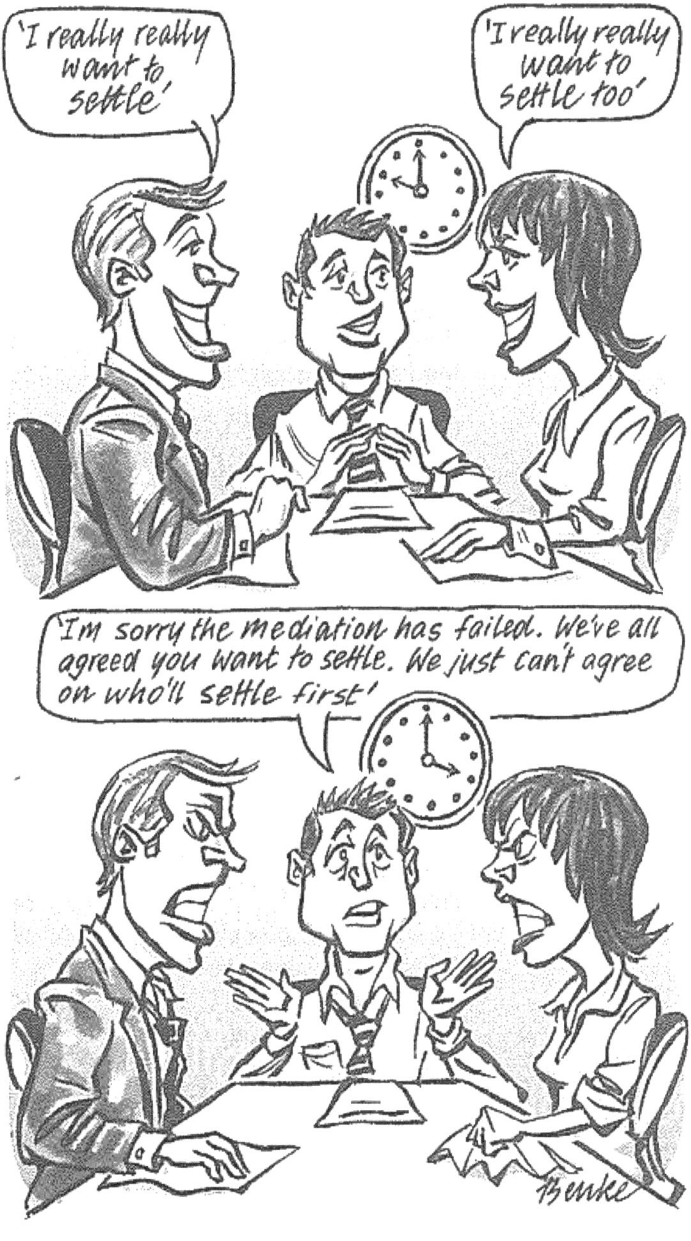

The Mediation Handbook: A practical guide for lawyers & participants in the art of mediation. First edition published in 2006.

Written by: John G Bolton

Illustration by: Joe Benke

Everything you won't learn
in books on Mediation.

At last! A handbook <u>not</u> for mediators.

An easy to follow, down-to-earth guide for lawyers (and for those participating in mediation) on the how, the why and the wherefore of mediation.

Includes a 29 point Checklist on all the things you need to do before the mediation starts.

'There is not a mediator in the business who does not use the costs of litigation as an inducement to obtain a settlement...'

'It is important that the decision makers be present at the mediation...'

'Practitioners need to understand that mediation is an invaluable process and properly prepared and conducted, can provide enormous advantage for the smart players in the serious game of litigation...'

'There is little point in mediating a dispute if all appropriate parties are not joined to the proceeding and are not at the mediation table...'

'Mediators are not magicians and they need cooperation from the parties and their legal representatives to bring about a satisfactory result...'

'When all else fails - walk out.'

ABOUT THE AUTHOR

John Bolton has over 36 years' experience in the practice of Law as a Barrister, Solicitor and Mediator operating predominantly in the areas of Commercial & Property Litigation including significant Building & Construction disputes.

He was admitted to practice in 1973 and signed the Bar Roll in 1975. From 1981 to 1983 he was engaged by the Hong Kong Government as Crown Counsel prosecuting Criminal Trials.

In 1993 he became accredited as a Mediator and conducted and appeared in many Mediations covering a broad range of disputes.

He regularly presented papers on Mediation to Solicitors, Barristers and Mediators and has published a number of articles on the topic in professional journals.

Now retired from his very active practice at the Bar, John is a Fellow of the Australian Institute of Company Directors. He has been an Associate Member of the Institute of Arbitrators and Mediators Australia, an Associate Member of the Chartered Institute of Arbitrators (UK), a member of the Victorian Bar Alternative Dispute Committee and President of the Building Dispute Practitioners Society.

CONTENTS

INTRODUCTION

"The full-scale trial can no longer be regarded as the paradigm method of dispute resolution, even for complex disputes involving subjects of high value ... alternative means of dispute resolution, conducted pursuant to the private agreement of the parties, can be expeditious, flexible and tailored to particular needs." Sir Gerard Brennan, former Chief Justice, High Court of Australia.

OVERVIEW

"I am yet to meet a person who, a year after settlement, is not happy with the fact the case was settled, no matter what the result." Author

Until the early 1990s it was often considered a sign of weakness if a litigating party made overtures to negotiate a settlement. It was also common to see groups of robed barristers outside the doors of various courts, busily trying to settle their cases at the last minute. Parties would hold their cards close to their chest in the hope of catching the other party off guard and last minute applications for adjournment with significant cost penalties were common.

We now practice in more enlightened times. Through the process of mediation, courts and tribunals have encouraged parties to mediate and an offer to negotiate is seen more as a sign of strength. Over 60% of all disputes are now settled well before the dreaded 'door of the court'. If they don't settle, at least the parties have had the opportunity to ventilate the issues and reduce the length of trials.

All mediations are different with no predictable results. All mediators are different and each has an individual approach. All those participating in mediations are different and have their own agenda.

I have set out in this handbook some approaches and tactics which may help lawyers appearing in mediations. None of my suggestions must be followed, in fact there will be circumstances where some of the approaches I refer to are inappropriate and should not be followed. But all of what is contained in this book should cause practitioners to think - about the process, about how to approach mediation, about the direction in which they want the mediation to proceed and about the result they want to achieve for their clients.

Most books and seminars about mediation are given from the mediators' perspective - how to be an effective mediator and how mediators should conduct mediations. In this handbook, mediation is approached from the point of view of the lawyers representing the parties and is to serve as a practical guide.

The aim of this book is to give legal representatives, be they solicitors or barristers, an insight into how they can best use the mediation process and mediators to resolve disputes for their clients, mitigate costs or improve the chances of success in court should the matter not settle.

Mediators may perceive some of my suggestions could make their task more difficult.

This is not my intention. I have endeavoured to provide food for thought for those practitioners who want to use the mediation process to their clients' best advantage and who are open to resolving the dispute.

My earnest belief is all practitioners have an obligation to approach mediation with a will to settle and should never attempt to obstruct the mediator or the process.

Mediation exists within the context of a culture of alternative dispute resolution which has grown in strength within the legal and broader communities to a point where this form of dispute resolution is now commonplace. Courts and Tribunals in Australia now refer most disputes to mediation as part of their normal process, reflecting the preference for early dispute resolution.

However many lawyers in mediations have never really considered how to maximise the process for their clients or for themselves. Nor have they, until now, any way of equipping themselves with sufficient knowledge to be effective players in the process.

Mediation is an art form which, if conducted properly, will resolve most disputes. At the very least the process will provide a valuable insight into the strengths and weaknesses of each party's case, setting the scene for eventual resolution or narrowing the issues in dispute.

It is only the most unusual litigant who does not want to settle a dispute on reasonable grounds. Invariably parties to litigation would rather have their lawyer supporting them through a meaningful, well conducted and structured mediation process than be mere spectators to a litigation grinding to an expensive and uncertain resolution.

I would like to thank both Mark Bolton B.Comm LLB and Neil McPhee LLM (Lond) for their support and contribution. The mistakes are all mine.

WHY MEDIATE

Information is power.

Mediation is now so commonplace that some practitioners take the process for granted and treat it with something akin to disdain. They may regard mediations as easy, not like trials where a barrister is briefed and preparation is extensive. After all, some will say, mediation requires little preparation, you can't lose a mediation and it's hard to make a fool of yourself no matter how badly prepared you are.

Practitioners need to understand that mediation is an invaluable process and properly prepared and conducted, can provide enormous advantage for the smart players in the serious game of litigation.

The purists tell us that mediations resolve disputes in a time and cost effective manner, free up courts, save everyone lots of money and give the parties involved ownership of the outcome leading to lasting settlements. You can't argue with that.

However there are other real benefits of the mediation process. Most, if not all, parties in mediation give it their best shot. How else can you convince your opponent to settle if you don't state your case with clarity and force and bring out all the facts and the legal arguments to bolster your case and mitigate the other party's?

You can get no better opportunity than at mediation to:

    a.   find out exactly what the case is against your clients;

    b.   see the whites of the other parties' eyes and assess what sort of witnesses they will make;

    c.   assess your own clients and their cases;

    d.   hear the legal arguments and learn of the cases that will be used against you; and

    e.   discover the other side's interpretation of the dispute.

Mediation should be treated with respect and the parties should enter the process prepared to settle the dispute. If that is not achieved, you should at least have obtained as much information as possible about the opposition and their case.

PRE-CONCEPTIONS

"Better cases than yours have been lost and worse cases than your opponents' have been won." Author

All parties to litigation want to settle - the only question is on what terms are they prepared to settle?

In many instances parties do not know what they will eventually be prepared to accept or pay until their resolve has been tested. What is finally accepted by way of settlement often takes into account a myriad of factors having possibly no direct relationship to the issues in dispute. These can include the health of the parties or their families, their finances, travel plans, business commitments, relationship with the other parties and how they have interpreted the advice given to them. In short, parties may want to settle for reasons which will never be apparent to their lawyers.

Accordingly, practitioners who have preconceptions about their clients' attitude to settlement, who do not give them every opportunity to settle and who stand in the way of a proper settlement, do their clients a great disservice.

Clients are entitled to make an informed decision. It is the obligation of every legal representative to study the case fully, give meaningful advice and provide the clients with a realistic appraisal of their chances of success, giving them as many options as possible to avoid litigation. It would be very embarrassing to tell your clients they have a strong case only to discover later you overlooked facts or law which prove highly detrimental to the case. If the clients choose not to settle and eventually lose, they should not be left feeling they did not receive full advice on all the possibilities and probabilities of the likely outcome.

It is easy to preconceive limitations on your clients' desire to settle. Some clients are vehement they will not settle for anything less than their stated 'bottom line'. It is often surprising to find these clients were simply trying to keep up a brave face, sound tough or had misunderstood their position. Once they have worked through the ups and downs of a mediation, you may well find some clients are prepared to settle happily at a level much less advantageous than they had first indicated.

Some clients want their lawyers to believe they will litigate no matter what, thinking the lawyer will then do a better job. This approach can give the lawyer a distorted idea of what the clients will accept by way of settlement. You should keep an open mind to the possibilities of settlement and what your clients will eventually find acceptable and you should ensure your clients do likewise.

There are no sensible lawyers in practice who will guarantee a result for their clients. Whenever you are confronted by opponents who claim their clients cannot lose, try suggesting they put it in writing. Not surprisingly, no one seems to take up the offer. The uncertainty of litigation is a compelling enough reason for anyone to settle.

MEDIATING IN GOOD FAITH

"In my view the expectation of good faith can be no more than an expectation or a hope." Sir Laurence Street

There is often talk of mediating 'in good faith' and certainly the parties to mediation should conduct themselves in such a way to ensure they do not abuse the process or frustrate the Court or Tribunal or the other parties.

Some mediators include a clause in their mediation agreements to the effect the parties agree to mediate in good faith. But how do you enforce such an agreement and what is the loss in the event of a breach?

Given 'good faith' is a matter of perception, what could be done by the mediator or, for that matter, the other parties, if one party is perceived not to act in 'good faith'? I suspect not much. Only the clearest breach of an obligation to mediate in good faith could lead to a successful action, but without an admission how would you prove it? In any event the quantum of damages for such a breach, if there in fact be any loss, would be difficult to assess. It is unlikely the offending party would be ordered to return to mediation and make a better fist of looking like they are acting in good faith.

It is every party's right to negotiate in whatever way they see fit. If you believe your clients are not acting in good faith you might consider advising them they are missing out on an opportunity to settle the matter and urge them to change their attitude. If they don't agree then you ought to advise them to conclude the mediation and have the mediator wrap it up. If you perceive the other parties are not acting in good faith, discuss the matter with the mediator. If the problem persists, cut your losses and simply bring the mediation to an end.

As Tony Fitzgerald QC said 'The object of mediation is to resolve disputes not to start a fresh dispute as to whether or not there is an enforceable obligation to negotiate in good faith.'[2]

1.   IAMA News Dec 2005 p.16
2.   IAMA News Dec 2005 p.17

BEFORE MEDIATION

APPROACHES TO MEDIATION

"Thinking is the hardest work there is, which is probably the reason why so few engage in it." Henry Ford

The nature of any mediation is as different as the personalities of the participants. It is vital in the conduct of mediations to focus on the desires of all the parties to reach settlement.

Approach mediation after having reflected on ways to bring the dispute to resolution. Include in your reflection a consideration of all issues which may have an impact on the result - who should be the mediator; your clients' particular needs or weaknesses; what you know of the other parties and their lawyers; what you consider would be an acceptable result given the particular circumstances of the case.

You should engage a skilled mediator who has the ability to accommodate the range of personalities around the table. The mediator's role is to assure the fairness of the process, facilitate communication, maintain the balance of power between the parties and, most importantly, crunch a deal.

A powerful weapon in any mediation is simply thinking -thinking about your case, the opposing case, what your clients want, what the other party will accept, why there is a dispute, what might end the dispute and how you can best achieve closure.

Human nature being what it is the vast majority of people want to avoid conflict. In testimony to the effectiveness of mediation, results indicate at least two-thirds of disputes settle at mediation and a significant proportion of the remainder settle before court.

All litigation carries with it a loss of control and a degree of risk, sometimes resulting in high financial and personal cost to the parties. Settling on acceptable terms is obviously preferable, particularly if the parties need to continue their business or personal relationships into the future.

THE BENEFITS OF MEDIATION

"It is better to have settled than to have lost." Author

There is no such thing as a case which cannot be lost, nor, it would appear, is there such a thing as cheap litigation. Both of these truths form the basis of settlement in most mediations.

The benefits of mediation are many and should be explained to your clients early in the litigation process. These include:

a.   legal costs are minimised and contained;

b.   the uncertainty of litigation is removed;

c.   the interests of the parties, beyond legal and factual issues, are taken into consideration;

d.   communication between the parties can be had in an optimistic and rational environment;

e.   there is scope to explore creative and lateral solutions in a constructive manner;

f.   the parties make their own decisions and maintain control;

g.   ownership of the outcome assists in a lasting resolution;

h.   the process is relatively speedy, certainly compared with Court proceedings;

i.   publicity is minimised and the process can be confidential; and

j.   you can assess the strengths and weaknesses of your clients' case and of the other parties.

CHOICE OF MEDIATOR

The choice of mediator is very important to the chances of settlement:

a. choose a mediator who is persistent and who will not allow the parties to abandon the mediation until absolutely all avenues have been investigated and exhausted. Persistence is often the single most important attribute of a mediator;

b. choose an accredited mediator but understand accreditation alone does not mean the mediator is experienced or skilful;

c. look for a mediator who takes pride in a job well done and in settling disputes;

d. find a mediator who has insight into the problems of litigation;

e. a skilful mediator does not necessarily have to be a specialist in the subject of the particular dispute, although in some areas it may be preferable;

f. understand the best mediators are intuitive. They are also patient and friendly and good listeners;

g. the mediator should have the personality and ability to convince parties of the benefits of a settlement;

h. a skilled mediator should have the ability to bring closure to the process; and

i. find a mediator with the ability to exert enough pressure to ensure all parties at least arrive at their respective bottom lines before the mediation is concluded.

A good mediator should be able to reduce the levels of animosity between the parties.

Find a mediator with the ability to be creative and think laterally and offer a full range of reasons to settle and provide alternatives to litigation.

Once found, a skilful mediator should be recommended in future mediations.

WHEN TO MEDIATE

The best time to mediate is:

    a.   before legal costs have become an issue;

    b.   before the parties have become too entrenched to settle comfortably;

    c.   before the legal process causes too much animosity between the parties;

    d.   after all issues have been identified; and

    e.   after all possible parties have been joined to the litigation.

The best time to mediate often depends on the dispute, the parties and their lawyers. Mediate too early and you risk not having identified all issues or not having all parties at the table. Mediate too late and the costs may have escalated to the point where the only way out is to proceed to judgment. In a particularly complex matter there may be no one ideal time and the parties may need a number of mediations before resolution is achieved.

In almost all disputes mediation should occur as early as possible and it is better to mediate too early than too late.

Remember an early mediation allows time before the case is heard for another mediation to take place or at least to engage in further negotiations.

Mediations are cheaper than trials and you can have as many mediations as the parties wish but, generally, you can have only one trial.

PRE-MEDIATION AGREEMENT

A pre-mediation agreement is important to define the parameters of the mediation.

Each mediator is likely to have their own style of agreement, but each agreement should contain some basic matters. Ensure the agreement deals with all appropriate issues and is signed by all persons who ought to be bound by its terms.

Although common law principles of 'without prejudice' negotiations and the various Rules of Court cover mediations, the question of confidentiality is not clear. The pre-mediation agreement should provide for the mediation to be confidential.

A settlement is generally reached when one party makes an offer and the other party accepts it. A settlement does not need to be in writing nor does it have to be signed before a binding settlement is reached. For a mediation to have the best chance of success the parties should feel free to say whatever they want without fear of being ambushed and having the other side claim an offer was made and accepted and the matter is therefore settled. In any event, without written terms of settlement the potential for further dispute is obvious.

Accordingly the pre-mediation agreement should also provide the mediation process is not settled until written terms of settlement are signed by the parties to the mediation.

If the mediator has not provided an adequate pre-mediation agreement, there is no reason why you should not insist on one. At least send a letter to all parties and the mediator making clear the basis upon which your clients will attend the mediation.

CONFIDENTIALITY

"The best kept secrets are the ones that aren't worth telling." Author

What is discussed in mediation should be on a 'without prejudice' basis and should not be used in the trial of the action. However 'without prejudice' does not mean it is confidential. To avoid any arguments about the status of what is discussed have the parties attending the mediation agree to confidentiality at the outset.

An agreement in writing which provides the mediation is being conducted in confidence helps put everyone at ease and encourages a free exchange of ideas and information. It also puts all parties on an even footing. The confidentiality agreement should include all those who may be present at the mediation, including those who are not parties to the action.

If the mediator has not included such a clause in the mediation agreement, you should send a letter to the mediator and the other parties confirming this aspect and any other issues of concern to you.

NOT SETTLED UNTIL SIGNED

"There's many a slip 'twixt cup and lip."

It is important for the parties to agree before the mediation commences, the dispute is not settled until written terms of settlement are signed.

To avoid further dispute, the parties need to have all issues resolved and in writing before a settlement is finalised. If one party claims the matter has settled verbally, enormous embarrassment and uncertainty can be caused if their claim is at odds with other parties' understanding.

Those involved in mediation, including the lawyers, should feel free to discuss all matters openly and not be concerned with falling into deals they may regret.

Often it seems the process of drawing up acceptable terms of settlement takes longer than actually arriving at the 'settlement'. When the settlement terms are put into writing the issues tend to become crystalised and one or other party may realise they did not fully understand the deal or insist on a term that had not been previously discussed or considered.

Agreeing the matter is not settled until written terms of settlement have been signed has a number of advantages:

a. the parties are more relaxed about discussing matters with each other and are more likely to make concessions knowing that they will not be bound by those concessions until they are put into writing;

b. misunderstandings during the mediation are avoided; and

c. the parties can move towards settling the big issues leaving the technical points for later.

PRE-MEDIATION CONFERENCES

A pre-mediation conference between the mediator and the various legal representatives is good practice, especially in the larger and more complex matters. During the conference the mediator and the lawyers are given the opportunity to discuss their requirements to ensure the mediation will proceed smoothly on the designated day and avoid the possibility of adjournment or abandonment. At the conference you should:

a. clarify the terms on which the mediator is engaged;

b. identify who will be attending the mediation;

c. ensure all parties have in attendance someone with unlimited authority to settle;

d. ensure the real decision makers will attend the mediation;

e. request from the other side any documents, reports or information that will be needed to facilitate a meaningful process;

f. agree on matters such as confidentiality and settlement requiring written and signed terms;

g. ensure the particulars and quantum of the claim are provided; and

h. identify and attempt to resolve any matters that may interfere with the smooth running of the mediation.

WHO SHOULD ATTEND THE MEDIATION

The mediation process itself is important to the mediation's success and throughout it there is often a range of emotions and pressures that affect the participants. Skilled mediators should be able to apply a series of pressures on those present to encourage them to abandon any pre-conceived 'bottom line' and move towards settlement.

Those attending the mediation are given the opportunity to assess each side's case. They get a feel for the negotiations and are in a position to observe the subtleties of the process. All of these important factors, which form the basis of the decisions to be made, are lost to those who do not attend the mediation.

The decision maker in any given matter may be someone other than the party named in the proceeding - perhaps the wife, husband or partner of a party, a particular director or number of directors of a company or the claims manager of an insurer.

It is important that the decision makers be present at the mediation. If they are not they will not be subjected to the process and will not have the understanding that comes with having taken part in the mediation. There is also a risk that the party attending may be reluctant to settle on acceptable terms simply for fear of having to later explain their reasons for settling to the absent decision maker. In the absence of the decision maker, those attending are more likely to choose to not settle. Contact by telephone does not replace the effect of being present throughout the complete process.

For mediation to be effective you should always ensure all decision makers, both those of your clients and the other parties, are present during the entire mediation.

PREPARATION

PREPARE YOUR CASE

"Forewarned is forearmed; to be prepared is half the victory." Miguel de Cervantes

Has your case been pleaded fully? There is little point in attempting mediation if you have not identified at least the main issues in the dispute you are trying to settle.

It sounds inherently weak to claim, during the running of a mediation, that you will be filing a counterclaim or joining some other party if the matter does not settle.

If your clients have a strong claim, then plead it. If your clients' claim is not strong, then plead it anyway and make it look strong. If other parties should be joined, then join them. And do it before you mediate.

If an expert's report is needed to support your clients' case, make sure you have obtained it as early as possible prior to the mediation and make it available to the other parties. Producing an expert's report for the first time at the mediation may only frustrate the process. The opposition would be entitled to have scant regard for a late served report and it may cause the mediation to be adjourned until they have had their expert consider it.

Quantify the claim. There is little point in trying to settle a dispute over money if you do not know how much your clients want to be paid or are prepared to pay. If you are acting for the defendant and the plaintiff has not quantified the claim adequately then insist that they do so in sufficient time to allow you to consider it. Conversely, if you want your opponents to give full consideration to your clients' claim, make sure you provide them with a proper quantification of it.

The other parties are unlikely to cave in and settle on your terms unless confronted by some real reasons why they should do so. Show them they are at real risk if they do not settle. If you don't do this they may not come to grips with your clients' position and make the necessary allowances.

A well-documented and calculated claim has a significant effect on the opposition. It says clearly you are thoroughly prepared and mean business. It tells the other side you are ready to run the case immediately and are happy to have the matter set down for trial at the earliest possible time if settlement is not achieved. Parties faced with the prospect of a trial soon after mediation, at a time when they may not be fully prepared, are more likely to make concessions they otherwise would not make.

If you can't plead your clients' case before mediation you should at least gather as much information as possible to support the claim and articulate it in a Position Statement. Putting your clients' case in writing will at least clarify its strengths and weaknesses for you and give the other side the opportunity to explore and understand your position.

JOIN ALL PARTIES

'The more the merrier'

There is little point in mediating a dispute if all appropriate parties are not joined to the proceeding and are not at the mediation table. Mediation without all appropriate parties present often ends in farce with those present invariably suggesting that the absent party should be contributing to the settlement.

Are the parties to the litigation the correct parties? During the mediation is too late to discover the incorrect parties are suing or being sued. Make sure you have carried out all appropriate checks.

Have all the appropriate parties been joined? If there are parties who should properly be joined they should be present to enable all matters to be resolved.

One of the greatest causes of failed mediations is the absence of a relevant party. If it is proper to join other parties, then join them. The more parties involved the more money will be at the table and usually the better the chance of settlement.

PREPARE YOURSELF

"Chance favours only the prepared mind." Louis Pasteur

There is no substitute for thorough preparation of a case and your part in it. Mediation is often embarked upon early in litigation so allow yourself as much time as possible for preparation, obtain clear and full instructions and make sure you are fully prepared. There should be no excuses.

Get your facts right. During the open session of the mediation you will need to be able to answer questions or correct misconceptions. Doing so will immediately indicate whether you are fully prepared or not. If you are not prepared, apart from embarrassing yourself, you risk your clients' case looking weak, which in turn will empower the other side.

Your clients will know less about the law than you - at least you would hope so. But they will have an intimate knowledge of the facts, will expect you will too and will know if you make a mistake.

Most mediators will want to use the cost and length of the eventual trial to persuade the litigants to settle. You will need to give consideration to the duration of the proceedings, ascertain the costs to date and make a realistic calculation of the future costs.

There is no case you cannot lose. You need to assess the chances of success or failure for your clients. This may be difficult but your clients will want to know. There is no point in predicting overly optimistic outcomes unless you are prepared to guarantee them - and you won't be.

CLIENTS' EXPECTATIONS OF YOU

"Perception is reality." Lee Atwater

In my experience the best way to approach any mediation is to look at yourself through your clients' eyes. What do my clients expect from me? This should be the first question. Of course barristers need to factor into the equation what their instructing solicitors expect as well.

It is reasonable for a lay person to believe that their lawyers know the law. This seems hardly surprising. Any indication to the contrary is not a good start.

The clients, having taken for granted that your knowledge of the law is without bounds, expect that you also have an unlimited knowledge of the facts of their case. That is one thing that the clients know a lot about and you will be expected to have obtained appropriate instructions from your clients and other witnesses and be fully conversant with the issues before the mediation commences.

The more facts at your disposal, the better able you will be to represent your clients and the better result you will obtain - and the more skillful you will appear.

If your clients' case is strong, and you have articulated it properly, the other side is more likely to see sense and settle on reasonable terms. If your clients' case is weak then you will need to present it in such a way that it appears strong. Naturally, if you present your case poorly or in an unconvincing manner you may well jeopardise an acceptable settlement.

ADVISE YOUR CLIENTS ABOUT THE COSTS AND LIKELY OUTCOME

"I was never ruined but twice; once when I lost a lawsuit and once when I won one." Voltaire

You will need to tell your clients what they have spent and what they are likely to spend on the case. They should have a reasonable understanding of the costs they will incur if they win and the costs they may be ordered to pay if they lose. There is no point being overly optimistic - be realistic.

Give your clients an appraisal of their chances of success or failure and discuss the options for settlement. It is too late to wait until after the clients have lost the trial to tell them you thought they would lose. If that is the case they should know as soon as possible.

Advise your clients of the anticipated duration of the proceedings and the likely costs. There is no mediator in the business who does not use the spectre of legal costs and the uncertainty of litigation as a big stick to bring about a settlement. During mediation you can expect the mediator will ask the parties to calculate the costs of the litigation and, as often is the case, may settle on an exaggerated figure. If your clients have been given a realistic appraisal of the costs they won't panic, unlike the party who has not been so advised.

Keep your clients concentrated on 'commercial reality' and on resolving the dispute on terms which take into account the costs and uncertainty of litigation, sleepless nights, disruption to their businesses and the possible ignominy of defeat.

At this stage you may also take the opportunity to advise your clients about the use and effect of offers of compromise.

ADVISE YOUR CLIENTS ABOUT THE MEDIATION PROCESS

"Court is where principles go to die." Author

There is no harm using the mediation process as an opportunity for a little self-promotion and to impress clients with your knowledge. Your clients probably know nothing about using mediation yet this structured negotiation process generally follows a fairly standard path.

Start by telling clients what you expect the mediator will say and what will probably happen.

Mediators should tell the parties that:

    a.   they are not judges and will not decide any issues;

    b.   they will not give legal advice;

    c.   the process is confidential;

    d.   anything said to the mediator in private session will not be divulged to the other party without permission;

    e.   the process is 'without prejudice' and any admissions cannot be used at the trial; and

    f.   the matter will not be settled until terms of settlement are signed.

You should advise your clients that:

    a.   one party, normally the plaintiff, will give its version of the dispute first and the other party will respond;

    b.   their legal representative will probably do the talking;

    c.   they will hear the strengths and weaknesses of each side;

    d.   the other parties will be claiming they will win and your clients will lose;

    e.   the mediator may ask them to outline their case but they can defer to their legal representative if they prefer;

    f.   they do not need to say anything, but if asked a question they can answer it themselves or defer to their lawyer to answer;

    g.   if they want to they can make a statement to the other parties;

h.   they should not be cross examined (you will object to any attempt to cross examine your clients);

i.   it is their mediation;

j.   they can leave the mediation at any time;

k.   they do not have to settle; and

l.   each party is expected to be civil to the other.

If your clients are put at ease, and you are seen to be right about the procedure that will be followed, it is a great start to earning your clients' respect. When the time comes to advise them whether or not to settle, they are more likely to agree with you.

Your clients should understand that the day may be a long one, and they should take the necessary steps to avoid allowing the pressures of a lengthy process to get to them. You might suggest your clients treat the process as an 'experience in life' and spend some of their time observing the different personalities and body language around the table.

Explain to your clients they will probably feel a wide range of negative emotions - anger, disappointment and frustration -but advise them to hang in there, sit back and enjoy the show!

You ought also to factor into the equation the tactics you expect the other side to adopt. How will the other parties behave? Is your opponent the type to come in with all guns blazing, thump the table, proclaim that your claim has no merit and your clients will lose? Or is your opponent likely to be the quiet but ruthless type, overbearing the proceedings with facts and law? If your clients are not forewarned, your opponent's behaviour may unnerve them and make you look unprepared.

Discuss these possibilities and provide an understanding of what might occur allowing your clients the opportunity to appreciate the theatre of the process rather than be unsettled by it.

There should be as few surprises for your clients as possible.

THE LENGTH OF THE MEDIATION

"We're lost, but we're making good time!" Yogi Berra

Rushed mediations are often unsuccessful. Ample time should be allowed to enable all issues to be canvassed and explored. Often the longer time allowed for mediation the better the chances of success. Attitudes change during mediation and what may be an inflexible view point at the commencement is often considerably mellowed after a few hours of negotiation.

Generally the more time the parties have to negotiate the better the outcome. All issues need to be canvassed even if they are simply matters concerning only one party and appear irrelevant to the overall dispute.

Each case is different and you ought to give some thought to the period of time that should be made available to enable the dispute to be properly mediated. There is no point booking a mediator for a half day mediation if there are clearly many complex issues to be resolved or there are several parties involved.

One of the most powerful attributes of a mediator is persistence and mediators should be afforded the opportunity to be persistent. Limiting the time available may deny the parties the chance to settle.

THE USE OF EXPERTS IN MEDIATIONS

"'X' is an unknown quantity and a spurt is a drip under pressure."

Some disputes require the use of expert evidence to resolve issues between the parties.

It may be helpful to have experts attend to help resolve some of the technical or complex issues. It is unlikely that having only one party's expert attend will be of much assistance unless the other side has sufficient expertise itself to deal with the situation.

If you think that expert evidence may assist in resolving the dispute communicate this to the mediator and the other parties well before the mediation is to take place and suggest that all appropriate experts attend to attempt a resolution of any areas of disagreement between them.

Of course there is no point in having experts attend if their reports have not been made available to the other parties in sufficient time to enable the other side's experts to give them some consideration.

DURING THE MEDIATION

THE MEDIATION ENVIRONMENT

"'Will you walk into my parlour?' said the Spider to the Fly,
'Tis the prettiest little parlour that ever you did spy.'" Mary Howitt

The physical environment in which mediation is held can have a significant impact on the way matters proceed.

It is preferable, but not vital, the mediation takes place in neutral territory. Much successful mediation is conducted in the rooms of one of the party's solicitors or barrister. However there are many reasonably priced and neutral mediation facilities available.

Clearly mediation should be conducted in comfortable surroundings with sufficient break out rooms to enable the parties to discuss matters in private. A white board with the appropriate pens and erasers in each room is invaluable as is adequate communication and office equipment.

I noticed in a book on how to conduct mediations, written for mediators by a highly experienced mediator, various drawings of the positions the author suggested participants should take up around the mediation table. Several options were described but each had the lay people closest to the mediator and within the mediator's sphere of influence, next in line were the solicitors and furthest away the barristers. What the author was setting out was what best suited the mediator. He placed himself closest to the people over whom he wanted to exert the most influence and those who were potentially the greatest threat to his control, the lawyers, were placed as far away as possible.

Personally, unless a lawyer has proved to be a nuisance or is attempting to scuttle the mediation (a rare occurrence) my approach as a mediator is to involve the lawyers as much as possible and use their skills and authority to help settle the matter. The lawyers have the most influence over their clients and, if I am mediating, I am not concerned if the lawyers sit near me. As mediator I prefer to give the lawyers some ownership of the process and any attempt to exclude them may make it less likely they will be happy to assist. As mediator I try to involve the skill and knowledge of the lawyers and get them on my 'settlement team'.

I believe it best for the legal representative to be next to the mediator and if there are two, they should sit either side of the clients. This way the mediator's influence over your clients is defused and your clients have the comfort of some protection from the opposing side. It is important for clients to have their legal advisers in the thick of it and the position of the lawyers should be such that the clients are not feeling exposed to the influence of the other side's lawyers.

Body language is an important part of the negotiating process and the mediation is probably the first opportunity for your team to show the other side you mean business, so be prepared to behave appropriately.

Some books on negotiation suggest you take up a position of power at the table - sit with your back to the light forcing your opponents to look at the glare, or sit at the head of the table. But remember, as the real negotiation in mediation is generally conducted in 'private session' after you have left the mediation table and in the absence of the other parties, these 'power positions' may have little effect.

Mediators, after having introduced the process, normally ask the legal representatives to summarise their clients' position and then ask their clients if they would like to add anything before moving to the next party. Some mediators seek to have the parties explain their respective cases themselves. If you have discussed this possibility with your clients before the commencement of the mediation they will be ready to handle the situation.

Having your clients state their case may have the benefit of allowing them to appear resolute and to speak their minds. However, if your clients are not sufficiently articulate to carry this off it could put them under significant pressure and they may make mistakes.

THE LAWYER'S ROLE

As indicated earlier, you should ensure the mediator states in opening the mediation, and the other parties acknowledge:

a.   the process is confidential;

b.   anything that is said is 'without prejudice'; and

c.   the matter is not settled until terms of settlement are signed.

It is important for all present at the mediation to feel absolutely free to say anything constructive and this feeling is enhanced if all parties are signed up on these three points. Although there may be rules of Court governing some of these matters, not all mediations are conducted by order of the Court. You will want to avoid any embarrassment that can occur if the other party takes a contrary stance and the mediator should ensure agreement is reached before the process commences. It is better to be safe than sorry.

Protect your clients from being cross examined and ensure they are not intimidated or abused in any way.

Take notes of what the other side claims about their case and your case. Take particular note of any issues that may require further investigation or research if the matter fails to settle and proceeds to trial.

The parties should be alert to the risks of verbally agreeing to accept an offer before they have had the opportunity of reflecting fully on its implications. There are cases where a party has verbally accepted an offer only to discover there has been a critical misunderstanding of its full terms and the other party has sought to enforce the agreement. This will not be a concern where there is agreement on the need for written signed terms before settlement can be achieved.

Sometimes, agreeing on and drafting the terms of settlement takes longer than reaching the actual 'settlement'. Certainly terms of settlement, other than simple ones, can raise issues that were not in the minds of the parties when the matter was 'settled' and it is only when the terms are put into writing these matters surface.

Keep a written record of all offers made and received paying particular attention to any special conditions. It is interesting how a review of the various offers and counter offers can often provide an insight into where the negotiations are headed.

Make sure the mediator understands your offers when you convey them and they are, in turn, being accurately conveyed to the other parties. Also make sure you fully understand the other parties' offers and have them clarified if necessary.

LOOK AFTER YOUR CLIENTS

"Your livelihood may depend on it." Author

You need to look after your clients throughout the mediation process. Often clients feel exposed and ill at ease during mediation and it is your role to help them overcome these feelings.

Looking after your clients has a number of positive effects and your clients will be more relaxed and should be able to give better consideration to the negotiations. Hopefully the result will be after settlement they will more likely remain content with what has occurred. If your clients are calm there is a better chance of an acceptable resolution but if settlement does not occur they will at least appreciate your efforts.

Before the mediation commences your clients will need to know that:

a. they are empowered and it is their mediation;

b. they can leave at any time - they are not trapped;

c. they do not have to settle;

d. the mediator cannot order them to do anything;

e. the mediator is not a judge;

f. the mediator is there only to facilitate a settlement;

g. the other side's lawyers are not entitled to cross examine them;

h. they do not need to say anything to the other side;

i. what is said will be confidential; and

j. the matter will not be settled until they have signed written terms of settlement.

THE MEDIATION PROCESS

Generally the mediation process follows a structured pattern and moves through the following stages, with the mediator alternating between the parties after they have moved into private session:

a.   resolution of any preliminary concerns;

b.   explanation of the process to the parties;

c.   acknowledgement of the needs and interests of all parties;

d.   identification and exploration of all issues;

e.   investigation of the claims;

f.   generation of creative options;

g.   evaluation of options;

h.   negotiation;

i.   exploration of commercial solutions and outcomes;

j.   verbal settlement; and

k.   written terms of settlement.

AUTHORITY TO SETTLE

"I have full unlimited authority to settle on my terms." Author

There is often little to be gained at mediation when one party does not have full authority to settle the dispute. All issues relating to authority to settle should have been resolved at the pre-mediation conference or otherwise before attending the mediation.

Before the mediation gets underway you should enquire whether the representatives of the other parties have full authority to settle. If they do not, make your displeasure known. It will be your call as to what to do next and the particular circumstances will determine whether you continue with the mediation or seek to have it adjourned.

If the decision maker or a person with unlimited authority cannot attend on behalf of your clients (you may be acting for an insurer or your clients may be unavailable) make the other parties aware of the situation well before the date set for the mediation. The mediation may need to be adjourned until all parties are available. Alternatively provide the person attending with an appropriate signed letter of authority to negotiate and sign terms of settlement.

THE COSTS OF LITIGATION

"To litigate is fine but to settle is finer." Author

The unfortunate fact is that litigation is expensive and it is not unknown for legal costs to outstrip the actual quantum of the claim. This is why mediation is so useful and why the process has been embraced by all who are involved in litigation -courts, parties and lawyers.

There is not a mediator in the business who does not use the costs of litigation as an inducement to obtain a settlement.

Mediators invariably use the legal costs issue as a big stick and often ask each party for an estimate of the eventual hearing time for the case. The parties tend to put forward the longest time frame possible to show the other side they are fearless and have so much evidence to call in support of their case it will take many days to get through it. If they don't suggest an appropriate duration of the trial, the mediator will. The other parties rarely disagree and soon you may have a five day trial estimated to take three weeks. An estimate of cost of preparation and the trial costs is then made. These figures are faithfully written on a white board by the mediator and the parties left to contemplate the sum. It is often possible to reach a six-digit figure in even the simplest cases. The effect is often interesting to watch and eventually the numbers seem to pulsate.

Of course, this will have little effect on your clients if you have warned them of what might happen and provided a realistic appraisal of the duration of the trial and its likely cost. If the mediator has written an inflated figure on the whiteboard in a room that your clients occupy, it's a good idea to rub it off when the mediator leaves the room.

Even an accurate appraisal of costs and time is likely to cause the most hardened clients to squirm. In any event, despite the seemingly exaggerated figures on the white board, only very brave lawyers would guarantee to their clients the eventual length of the trial and costs will be less than what the mediator has calculated.

Your clients should be advised they will never recover all the costs of the litigation even if they win 100%. Without a winning offer of compromise to protect the clients on the question of costs, a recovery of 50% to 70% of solicitor-client costs is to be expected. Or put another way, even if your clients win they may have to pay 50% to 30% of their own legal costs.

EXERT SOME INFLUENCE

Exerting influence does not mean you become painful or pushy, or a control freak or a nuisance. An aggressive attitude may have its place in some mediations but is often counterproductive.

You should always appear confident. There is no point looking like you are about to lose. Remember, effectively you are horse trading.

Most mediators invite the parties around the table to introduce themselves before the mediation commences. Rather than leave it up to your clients to introduce themselves, introduce yourself first then introduce your clients and each other member of your team by name. This approach tends to set a scene in which your team will appear united and well prepared. Your clients will appreciate the situation and feel their needs are paramount. If the opposing lawyers have not bothered to learn their clients' names, and this happens, the other side is forced to introduce themselves and a small but early advantage is yours.

The mediator will give an introduction and a summary of the mediation process and should touch on all important matters that may relate to the mediation. However some matters may be overlooked and you should raise them immediately including:

a. the identity of all persons present in the room. If you are not sure who someone is, ask;

b. the authority of those present to settle;

c. an agreement that the process is confidential, particularly if non-parties are present;

d. an agreement that the matter is not settled until written terms are signed;

e. the amount of time available for the mediation and that no-one needs to leave early;

f. the production of any documents or reports from the other parties, or an explanation why they haven't been provided; and

g.   any other matters that may have been overlooked.

Mediation is not the place for cross examination. Direct communication with the other party should be avoided unless the permission of their legal representative is first obtained. This works both ways.

Don't let the opposing parties try to bully or unsettle your clients or cross-examine them. If any attempts of this sort are made, politely tell the offending party to desist and enlist the assistance of the mediator if necessary. If the behaviour continues you may decide to leave the room.

Many mediators try to involve the parties personally and have them put their case forward. This approach tends to break down barriers and allows the parties the opportunity to express themselves and articulate what they regard as the important issues. Allowing the parties to openly discuss their concerns may assist in the eventual resolution of the dispute. Sometimes a party simply by having their complaint heard, or having the opportunity of telling the other parties what they think of their behaviour, can be the catalyst for settlement.

However allowing your clients to express themselves in open session may have some detrimental effects. They may divulge something prejudicial, show themselves to be weak witnesses or expose some aspect of their case which does significant damage to their prospects of success, either at mediation or the subsequent trial.

Before the mediation commences, discuss with your clients whether they should address the other parties in the joint session. Assess their strengths and weaknesses and discuss with them what approach is to be taken. Not all clients are articulate and unless they can improve their position by appearing to be open and on top of their case, or you assess they need to express a grievance, recommend that when asked for a comment they simply defer to their legal representatives to outline the case.

Certainly do not allow your clients to be cross examined by the other side. As their legal representative it is your duty to ensure your clients are protected from such tactics and are allowed to appear in the best possible light. The other side may be keen to test your clients and see how well they stand up to cross examination - don't let them.

You should look after your clients at all times. If the clients are happy with how they are being represented they are more likely to think their lawyer has really understood their needs and done a competent job. All clients want to be represented by someone who is able to put their case in a forthright and capable manner. If you represent your clients with care and skill, they are more likely to accept your advice on settlement and to remain clients in the future.

YOUR RELATIONSHIP WITH THE MEDIATOR

Mediators are not magicians and they need cooperation from the parties and their legal representatives to bring about a satisfactory result. It is your duty to your clients and to the Court or Tribunal to assist the mediator, within the limits of your instructions, to resolve the dispute. Do not try to frustrate the process or the mediator. Although you may be armed with all manner of tactics to advance your clients' case, don't let them get in the way of a proper settlement.

If the chosen mediator does not appear to be up to the job at hand, don't let that fact scuttle the mediation. There is no reason why you should not assist the process and the mediator. However be careful not to be interfering and remember you do not know what the mediator is saying to, or being told by, the other parties, so your assessment of the mediator may be wrong.

To be effective, a mediator should earn the trust and respect of the various parties. All mediators want to achieve a settlement of the disputes they mediate and they probably do not care if one side gets a better result than the other or could have done better had they held out for more.

Although it is essential to cooperate with and not mislead the mediator or your opponents, you and your clients should be selective in the information that is divulged to the mediator. Give serious consideration to your approach when dealing with the mediator who may well focus on the party who appears to be weak or keener to settle. Initially, in the hope the mediator will put more effort into making the other parties move towards settlement, you may consider it is better to give the mediator the impression your clients are not going to readily make concessions.

Mediators are only human and, although they should always keep the confidences you have entrusted to them, their body language, what they say and how they say it, may give you helpful insights into the other party's attitude to the negotiations. You can learn a lot by 'reading' the mediator. Of course, as the other parties may also be 'reading' the mediator you should be careful your clients are not sending unhelpful messages themselves.

If you are going to take the approach of appearing resolute or difficult to deal with it is vital you tell your clients what you are doing and give them frequent reality checks to avoid any unrealistic expectations. Be careful your clients do not start to believe their case is stronger than it actually is. If that happens, you run the risk of them losing commercial reality and a proper settlement may be jeopardised. It is very difficult to justify a reasonable settlement if you have allowed your clients to expect an unreasonable one.

PARTIES ALONE WITH THE MEDIATOR

If the process is not advancing the way the mediator might like or the lawyers are obstructing settlement, the mediator may ask to speak to the parties alone without their lawyers being present.

There clearly are some cases in which the parties, under the guidance of the mediator, may benefit from a one-on-one confrontation to clear the air about some issue which is precluding a settlement. If your assessment of the situation is such that you consider leaving your clients alone with the mediator and the other party is a wise move, adopt it. A number of very satisfactory settlements have been brought about by such an approach. However this should be avoided unless you are entirely satisfied your clients have the ability to negotiate competently on their own and they clearly understand what to say and do and the risks involved.

You should advise your clients they do not have to be alone with the mediator and the other parties and they should do so only if they are entirely comfortable. If the mediator has asked to speak to the parties alone, find out why dealing directly with the lawyers and their clients together is not proving satisfactory.

You should not allow the parties to get together without their lawyers unless there is an agreement that no settlement is reached until the parties have an opportunity to confer with their respective lawyers and written terms of settlement signed. It is very difficult to retreat from inappropriate concessions after they have been made and even a non-binding agreement reached between the parties whilst they are alone can cause problems.

If your clients are alone with the other parties and the mediator there is the potential for real problems - the clients may say something that is regrettable; some fact may be alluded to which is highly prejudicial, inappropriate concessions might be made and a settlement may be discussed which is not in the clients' best interests. I have seen apparently hard-bitten street-wise businessmen make surprising and completely unwarranted concessions in these circumstances.

Clients are paying their lawyers good money to represent and protect them. Allowing the mediator to put the parties together without lawyers present may expose the clients to more pressure than is helpful.

The mediator has no right to insist on being left alone with the clients. If you are not comfortable with such a course being taken stand firm and refuse the request. Your clients will appreciate your support and your stance ought not to cause the mediation to fail.

Being alone with the parties without their lawyers can be a risky business for mediators too. It can provide scope for criticisms to be made about the mediator's behaviour if one party is not happy with the result.

NEGOTIATING

OFFERS

"I'll show you mine if you show me yours." Author (aged 10)

Making offers in mediation is generally done through the mediator after the open session has been completed. There are many approaches to making offers but a skillful mediator should be able to distill any offers the parties make and render them as palatable to the other side as possible removing much of the game playing in which the parties may indulge.

If you have properly prepared you should be able to make a well-considered and intelligent first offer.

Some parties try to avoid putting the first offer. If acting for the plaintiff they might put forward the particulars of the claim as their first offer and leave it up to the defendant to make a counter offer. If acting for the defendant they might take the approach, as the plaintiff has the carriage of the case, the plaintiff should start the ball rolling. A skillful mediator should be able to elicit some meaningful starting point from the parties. Canvassing opening offers in private session allows the mediator to defuse any problems about first offers before the mediation commences. Such sessions generally fit comfortably into the subsequent more formal open session and enable the mediator to gain the parties' confidence in a casual atmosphere. In such circumstances, the parties are less likely to resist putting an opening offer.

There seems to be a curious phenomenon whereby a considerable number of mediations are settled at roughly the halfway mark between the opening offers of the respective parties. It is important to do your sums before negotiations commence. Your first offer and your various counter offers should enable you to proceed in steps that will hopefully produce a satisfactory result for your clients. If your offer is too close to your 'bottom line' you run the risk of being 'wrong-footed' as the parties get closer to an acceptable figure.

Try to have some solid reason behind your offers - you may wish to drop the claim for interest, or abandon an item of claim. Your offers should have meaning, validity and strength. Some parties make offers with odd figures to show thought has been given to the offer. Rounded off figures can tend to give the impression the offer is 'ball park' or they are simply being 'commercially realistic'. I once had a client who was convinced successful offers always had a number 7 in them - it seemed to work!

Whatever your approach, don't just throw offers out without giving considerable thought to the other party's offer; what that offer means; and where your offer will place your clients in the serve and volley of negotiations.

It is also necessary to consider the effect of either responding quickly or otherwise delaying your counter offer. A rapid response does not necessarily give an indication you are anxious. In fact it often gives the impression you are negotiating with confidence and have decided the other party's last offer is not worth much consideration. If you are paying attention to the bidding, you may be able to gauge the likely range of the other party's counter-offer and tailor your offer accordingly.

The last stage of the negotiating process is often the most difficult. Many times the parties, having moved relatively close to resolution, refuse to budge any further. This is where mediators will use their skills and some lateral thinking to try to break the deadlock and cajole, laugh, reason, beg or do whatever is required to resolve the impasse.

Principles are fine but they can be terribly expensive.

COMMERCIAL REALITY

"Those are my principles. If you don't like them then I have others."
Groucho Marx

A phrase often used in mediation is 'commercial reality'. The concept of commercial reality is worth considering particularly when emotions and principles are forming a barrier to common sense and settlement.

Commercial reality dictates that the parties try to leave principles, emotions and other personal matters out of the equation and consider the cost to them of unavoidable anxiety, wasted time and money and the inherent risks and uncertainty of litigation.

Once this is understood, commercial reality is a powerful concept and can allow sense to be brought into the discussions without the loss of too much 'face'.

Ask your clients - Is it commercially realistic to continue litigation and face possible loss? Is it commercially realistic to spend valuable time in court when they could be running their business? Is it commercially realistic to jeopardise their health and business on a risky return? Is it smarter to settle the matter now and get on with life?

THE 'BOTTOM LINE'

"I will absolutely go no further - unless you make me."   Author

So-called 'bottom lines' tend to be meaningless, particularly if they have been set by clients early in the process. Parties who have set a 'bottom line' have provided themselves with a psychological barrier to going beyond that limit despite later being confronted with good reasons to do so.

You should advise your clients to keep their minds open to all reasonable offers of settlement and not to be locked in to a specific figure or set of circumstances too early in proceedings.

Mediators never want to hear a party's 'bottom line' unless it is absolutely reasonable and may bring about a settlement. Learning a party's 'bottom line' may simply mean that the mediator has to work harder to remove it.

Similarly, unless your clients' 'bottom line' is so reasonable that a settlement is almost assured, there seems little point in divulging this to the other parties until the line has been reached and has actually become your 'final offer'.

You should never mislead your opponents. In certain circumstances during negotiations it is sometimes advantageous to be able to tell them that you do not know the figure at which your clients would finally settle. Knowing your clients' bottom line may remove that possibility.

The mediator should put the parties under sufficient pressure to give settlement their best shot and the mediation should not conclude until the parties have been brought to their respective absolute bottom lines. Having achieved this the mediator can do little more.

EACH PARTY WALK AWAY

If the particular circumstances of the case permit, probably the easiest way for a mediator to settle the dispute is to have each party agree to walk away and bear their own costs. This involves the least loss of face and avoids the psychological barrier of one party having to give anything to the other, no matter how small. In many disputes pride and principle takes over from commercial reality and each party steadfastly refuses to 'cross the Rubicon' i.e. pay money to their opponent.

If you have a weak case and your clients look to be in the position of having to pay some money 'each party walk away' is a comfortable point at which you can aim. It is a frustrating position if your clients expect to collect.

Matters of principle often involve both parties refusing to pay the other any money and it may be impossible to get them over the line. There is often a psychological barrier to such a payment and in certain factual situations, walking away is the only viable option.

If the matter is settled on this basis, make sure the terms of settlement cover the situation fully. Ensure the terms of settlement contain an adequate form of release which takes into account the possibilities of other actions that may be brought by or against third parties and also includes any indemnities your clients may require.

SPLITTING THE DIFFERENCE

'Splitting the difference' is useful when the parties reach their respective 'final offers' and refuse to budge. Splitting the difference is a very helpful negotiating tool and often works.

Be careful you are not seduced into offering to split the difference when the other side has not indicated they are also willing to take this approach. Making an offer to split the difference may simply allow the other party to counter with an offer to split the difference your offer has just created.

A skilled mediator should be able to resolve impasses at the appropriate time and should look for opportunities to split the difference.

If you want to split the difference always discuss the offer with the mediator and give instructions that you do not want that offer to be taken as simply another concession from your clients. To avoid actually putting an offer of this sort you could convey to the mediator that your clients may look favourably on splitting the difference if the other party gives the same indication.

A mediator receiving indications that both parties are prepared to settle on this basis should announce the position to the respective legal representatives together and advise that settlement will proceed on that basis.

DRESSING UP YOUR OFFER

"...that which we call a rose by any other name would smell as sweet."
Shakespeare

Remember, it is not only the mediator who has to think laterally - you have to as well. When the negotiations are getting close to the point where the parties are digging in you may wish to dress up your offer by tacking on to it some imaginative approach. Some successful offers that have resolved disputes include making a tax deductible donation of the difference between the offers to a charity, buying the other party a holiday or providing a valuable service to the other party at little actual cost.

If you are acting for the defendant who is to pay money you may make your offer more acceptable by offering to pay no more money but to pay it within a short period of time, say seven days. If circumstances permit, the defendant may even write out a cheque for the entire sum offered and have the mediator present it to the other party on a 'take it leave it' basis.

Parties who are struggling to pay any more than they have already offered, but are keen to resolve the dispute, might consider offering more money but adding a condition that they be given significant time to pay or pay it in installments.

If you are acting for a party who is expecting to receive money then you may resolve any impasse by offering to receive payment on terms such as 30 days for part and six months or longer for the balance, or other such acceptable terms.

THE FINAL OFFER

"Never say never again." Ian Fleming (James Bond)

Never claim your last offer was your clients' final offer unless it was. All too often one side will claim the offer they just made was the 'final offer' intending to put pressure on the other parties. It often doesn't work, particularly if you make yet another 'final offer' ten minutes later.

Apart from the fact making bogus 'final offers' may be misleading, it weakens your clients' negotiating stance and when your clients finally make their real final offer, the effect is lost.

Your final offer should be just that - final.

This should not, however, stand in the way of a proper settlement. Having bona fide stated that your clients have made their final offer it would be unrealistic to refuse to negotiate further if the parties were actually very close to settlement. There is no loss of face if your clients have made their 'final offer' but later see the sense of making yet another offer. Splitting the difference between final offers is often successful.

WRITTEN OFFERS

If the negotiations become deadlocked and your clients have reached their genuine final offer, a useful approach is to set out that offer in a formal offer of compromise and serve it on the other side at the mediation. Such a document confirms your clients have reached the end of the negotiations. It also forces your opponents to explain to their clients the adverse impact this may have on costs if the matter proceeds to judgment for a sum less favourable than the offer. The offer of compromise should only be made if it is your clients' final offer and the mediation is all but ended. As such an offer needs to be open for a period of time to allow for its consideration and acceptance. A written offer of compromise would normally be made as you pack your bags and start for the door. Although making such an offer may cause the mediation to be adjourned, if the offer is in the ball park, it may well be accepted and the matter settled.

Whenever mediation fails to reach settlement it is always a good practice to serve an offer of compromise as soon after the mediation as possible. It shows your last offer was genuine and will give the other side cause to reconsider its position. It also gives some protection for your clients on costs.

It depends on the circumstances of each case but, in my opinion, serving written offers prior to mediation is generally inappropriate. In order to be effective an offer of compromise should be at or even below your clients' genuine bottom line. It will set a mark from which your clients will find it almost impossible to do better at mediation whereas your clients may well be able to settle on more favourable terms than their bottom line if no offer of compromise has been made.

THE WALK-OUT

"Parting is such sweet sorrow." Shakespeare

When all else fails - walk out.

This is not to be encouraged, but some clients seem to delight in being theatrical. The fact remains that 'walk-outs' can sometimes have a dramatic effect on removing a stalemate and they have worked. If this approach is used make sure the clients are believable and the process doesn't become a farce and severely damage their credibility. Having walked out your clients may have trouble walking back in.

If the other side stages a walk-out - let them. There is not much you can do about it apart from simply shaking your heads and packing up. If the lawyers for the party who walks out are still present and don't look like they are going anywhere, the walkout has probably been staged.

If the other party walks out, the best approach is to call their bluff and give the performance the respect it deserves - tell the mediator the mediation is over and start to leave yourself.

Generally some warning of a walk-out is given to the mediator and a skillful mediator should be able to stop it, keep the ship afloat and maintain the mediation on course.

THE SETTLEMENT

"Will you still love me tomorrow?" The Shirelles

People change their minds. Satisfactory settlements are hard enough to achieve at mediation, but unless the parties are 'signed up' on the day there is a real risk they will change their minds before terms of settlement are finally drafted and agreed upon. Once settlement has been reached do all you can to have terms drafted and signed before the parties leave the mediation and the influence of the mediator. Many proper settlements have fallen through simply because the terms of settlement were not resolved at the mediation and the parties were given the opportunity to reflect on the deal.

Given you are attending mediation with the intention of settling the dispute, it is always good practice to take with you a precedent of terms of settlement for reference once the matter reaches settlement and terms are to be drafted and signed. Choose a precedent which contains a broad release.

If, for some reason, concluded terms of settlement cannot be drafted at the mediation, it is good practice to draft 'heads of agreement' if only to identify the key areas of agreement. However given the possibility of disagreement on the finer points of the settlement, you should ensure such heads of agreement contain a clause to the effect that they are a guide only and are not binding and that a concluded settlement is not reached until terms of settlement have been drafted, approved and signed by all parties.

Before the clients sign the terms remind them that they do not have to settle and ensure that they have read and understood what they are about to sign.

AFTER THE MEDIATION

POST MEDIATION CONFERENCE

If settlement has not been reached at mediation it is invariably very helpful to have a post mediation conference with your clients and the rest of your team at a time when the events are fresh in everyone's minds. At such a conference you can reflect on your case and that of the other parties and decide about the further steps necessary to successfully litigate the matter.

With the aid of your notes taken during the mediation decisions can now be made on matters including whether you:

    a.   continue the negotiations;

    b.   make any further offers;

    c.   join other parties;

    d.   discontinue against any parties;

    e.   make amendments to pleadings;

    f.   request further pleadings from the other parties;

    g.   gather further evidence;

    h.   find other witnesses;

    i.   investigate and research any legal arguments that have been raised; and

    j.   make a formal written offer of compromise.

EVERY MEDIATION IS A WINNER

Roll up! Roll up!

Settlement is not the only measure of a successful mediation and there is no such thing as a properly conducted mediation that has failed.

The mediator, and the legal representatives, should not allow the mediation to conclude until the parties have reached their respective bottom lines. The resolve of parties should be tested to at least that point. As a consequence of this, after an unsuccessful mediation, each party should be in a position to immediately make a written offer of compromise based on their last offer - there should be nothing left in the pot.

Mediation should provide an insight into your clients' case and the other party's case. That insight should allow you to see the strengths and weaknesses of both sides and provide the opportunity to pursue settlement or prepare your clients' case in a way that will better facilitate victory.

Be alert to what the other side is saying about your clients' case and their own.

    a.   Have they raised a point that you had not seen before?

    b.   Are they aware of your weak point?

    c.   Have they identified your killer point?

    d.   Have you identified their killer point?

    e.   How have they explained their clients' position?

    f.   Should you join another party?

    g.   Have they made a slip and referred to a weakness in their case you had not previously contemplated? Can you now take advantage of that?

    h.   Is their version of the facts different and more believable than your clients' version?

    i.   How can you improve your clients' case?

Mediation generally occurs early in the litigation process and at a time when amendments can be made to your pleadings or further investigations can be carried out. But it is never too late to improve your case.

KEEP NEGOTIATING

"Hope springs eternal." Alexander Pope

If the mediation does not result in a settlement there is no reason why settlement talks cannot continue afterwards.

The mediator ought to offer to continue the talks, or at least be a conduit through which communications flow, and be available to bring the parties back together if there remains some hope of a settlement.

Try to keep the door open and leave the mediation with an offer to continue discussions. Before departing the mediation you could indicate that you will keep your last offer open for a period of time to allow the other party to give it further consideration. A written offer of compromise should achieve this.

Contact the mediator soon after the mediation and ask that an attempt be made to elicit a further offer from the other parties or have the mediator put a modified offer on behalf of your clients. The other parties may be regretting being unable to settle at mediation and any inducement to settle might bear fruit. Your clients may also have reconsidered their position and want to make another offer.

CONCLUSION

Well, where does all that leave us?

Mediation is here to stay and is likely to remain a corner stone of legal practice well into the future.

I hope you will have been sparked into thinking about the process of mediation, your role in it and how you can best use the process to serve your clients.

There is not necessarily any right way to mediate, but there are a number of wrong ways. The process is fluid, the players are forever changing and the issues to be resolved are as diverse as human nature.

Although settlement at mediation is generally the main object, mediation is a powerful tool and, when used properly, can provide beneficial outcomes even if settlement is not achieved. If you approach and run mediation with care you should have at least learnt more about the opposing case as well as your own and so be in a far stronger position to plan for the hearing. You ought to have gained a greater understanding of the facts and law relating to the dispute, greatly improved your client's chances of success and be in a commanding position to run the case to a successful conclusion.

Who could ask for anything more?

PRE-MEDIATION CHECKLIST

1. Have you prepared your case fully?

2. Do you have a sufficient understanding of the relevant law?

3. Do you have a sufficient understanding of the relevant facts?

4. Are the parties to the action the correct parties?

5. Have you joined all of the appropriate parties?

6. Have you provided the other parties with sufficient particulars of your claim or defence?

7. Have the other parties provided you with sufficient particulars of their claim or defence?

8. Have you sufficient particulars of the quantum of your clients' claim/counterclaim?

9. Have the other parties provided you with sufficient particulars of the quantum of their claims/counterclaim?

10. Have you requested the other parties produce any documents and, if so, have they been produced?

11. Have the other parties requested you produce any documents and, if so, have you produced them?

12. Have you obtained an expert's report and, if so, has it been provided to the other parties?

13. Have any of the other parties obtained an expert's report and, if so, have you obtained a copy?

14. Have you chosen a skilled mediator?

15. Have appropriate rooms been arranged for the mediation?

16. Has a pre-mediation conference been held with the mediator and the opposing legal representatives?

17. Has a mediation agreement been produced and, if so, has it been signed?

18. Does the mediation agreement cover all appropriate matters?

19. Have the parties agreed to confidentiality?

20. Have the parties agreed to the dispute being settled only on written terms of settlement being signed?

21. Are the appropriate representatives of:
    a. your client
    b. the other parties
    able to attend the mediation?

22. Are all the decision makers of:
    a. your client
    b. the other parties
    able to attend the mediation?

23. Do those attending the mediation on behalf of:
    a. your client
    b. the other parties
    have unlimited authority to settle?

24. Is a written unlimited authority to settle required for anyone attending the mediation?

25. Have you calculated the likely duration of the trial?

26. Have you calculated the likely costs of the litigation?

27. Have you considered the likely outcome of the litigation?

28. Have you advised your clients of the likely duration of the trial, costs and outcome of the litigation?

29. Have you advised your clients about the mediation process and what to expect in the mediation?

30. Have you discussed with your clients how they are to conduct themselves during the open session of the mediation and what statements they might make?

31. As silly as it might sound, are you able to introduce your clients using their first names?

www.ingramcontent.com/pod-product-compliance
Lightning Source LLC
Chambersburg PA
CBHW041105180526
45172CB00001B/115